Growing Up in Wartime

Growing Up in Wartime

The Stories of Phyllis Coles, a Teenager During the Battle of Britain

As told to Aden Lane

Copyright ©

All rights reserved. No portion of this book may be reproduced, copied, distributed or adapted in any way, with the exception of certain activities permitted by applicable copyright laws, such as brief quotations in the context of a review or academic work.

Map images are from Google Maps™ mapping service.

Copies of this book may be purchased from Amazon.

Contents

Preface	1
Geography - My memorable places	3

Before the War

My family	5
Early days	8
Starting school	9
Finding my feet	11
Granny's	14
Sundays	16
Hayes Common fire	18
Granny's again	18
Teatime	19
Christmas	20
Pantomime and the Santa Claus Grotto	23
Birthdays	23
May Queen	24
Sickness	26
Dancing	27
Games and activities	28
Outings	30

Wartime

War breaks out	33
School of Craft and Industrial Design	34
Getting by	35
Avoiding evacuation	37
The Anderson shelter	37
Fund raising	38
Waiting for the planes to return	39
Open House	40
The Leaves Green Dornier	42
Being bombed	44

Capturing the enemy	47
Exploring crash sites	48
Going out in wartime	49
Summer holiday	50
Starting work	51
Madame Isobel	52
Joining the ATS	54
The end of war	55

After the War

Warrington	57
Congleton	59
Keele	62
Moving on	64
Shorncliffe	66
Teaching	68
Leaving the ATS	70
More teaching	71
Roy	73
Courting and marriage	74
Pictures from my later life	78

Preface

Biggin Hill Memorial Museum tells the story of Britain's most famous fighter station through the personal experiences of those who served there, and the community that supported them. I volunteer there in order to share some of these stories, which are variously uplifting, astonishing, moving, humorous, and always fascinating.

So I was delighted to meet a sprightly lady of 96, Phyllis Coles, who visited us in June 2022 and took obvious delight in sharing her many stories of growing up in the local area and witnessing the Battle of Britain playing out over her head as a teenager.

When I suggested capturing these stories to make them available to a wider audience, she leapt at the opportunity to keep them alive for future generations.

So, I met Phyllis again, recorded her memories, and created a set of stories that tell her life's story in her own voice, through her childhood near Biggin Hill, experiencing the Battle of Britain at first hand, commuting to work in London in the midst of bombing raids, travelling around the country for the ATS (Auxiliary Territorial Service, the women's branch of the British Army), and finally meeting and marrying her husband Roy.

Her stories provide a very personal and fascinating view of what it was like during that period, not only highlighting key aspects of living through the war, but presenting quite a different world, without television, mobile phones and the other paraphernalia that we take for granted 80 years later.

Sadly, Phyllis has since passed away, and we are no longer able to listen to her stories from her own lips, but I hope this book will enable her memories to be shared with new generations, as she wanted, who might ask: 'What was it like in the Second World War?'

Aden Lane
November 2022

Geography - My memorable places (approx)

- Buchanan Castle
- Congleton
- Leicester
- Warrington
- Colchester
- Keele
- London
- Leaves Green
- Shorncliffe

Before the War

My family

I was born at Nash Farm, Keston, on the 23rd of November 1925. My parents were James and Grace Allard, and I had a brother Cecil, who we called Bubs, and a sister Betty, they were younger than me.

Three little angels. Me on the left, Betty and Bubs

My parents were in service; my Mum was a lady's maid, my Dad came back to being a gardener after the First World War, uncles and aunts were grooms and nannies in the big houses around the Keston area - that was their background.

My Mother, Grace Featherstone
(her maiden name)

My Father, James Allard

Dad was an infantryman in the First World War, I know he was fighting in the trenches, he was wounded twice. I've been out there and seen where he'd been fighting in the trenches, it must have been absolute hell. He never said very much about the First World War, I think he was shocked.

Dad was too old to serve in the Second World War. His job was gardening, and that was a very healing thing to do, you're growing things and they're gentle and they're living. He was a gardener at Fox Hill House, near where my Granny lived. Later on, he worked for Bromley Council, looking after the gardens and things like that.

He was also in the Home Guard, every evening he was out training with the other men. He was in uniform, and they had guns. It took quite a chunk of his life.

My Father is second from the left in the front row, with his mates from the West Kent Regiment in the First World War, 1914 - 1918

Dad's brother, Uncle Tom, was taken prisoner in the First World War and ended up in Russia, and he managed to escape and he walked back from there, and he got back home.

My Granny was in the cottage, and this man walked up the garden path and came into the house and said "hello Mum", and she just didn't recognise him, she said he looked totally just not Tom. He got food as he kept walking, and he kept walking in the right direction, and finally he walked home.

We lived in Westerham Road on the Keston side of Leaves Green, in a row of houses along the road from Keston

Church, on the left if you're facing the church, near where the road forks off to go to Downe, close to the aerodrome. My Granny lived in Priors Cottage at the bottom of Fox Hill in Keston, and lots of aunties were also around.

Early days

The earliest memory I have was when I was three or four years old, standing on Bromley South Station waiting for the train to Maidstone with my parents on a bright sunny morning, wearing a sky blue wool coat, trimmed with a grey fur collar and cuffs, which my Mum had made for me. I loved wearing it. My Grandmother (my Mum's Mother) must have died recently. I was looking up at a clear blue sky with a small white cloud sailing across it and I asked whether Granny was in it going up to Heaven. I remember it very clearly.

I don't remember this Grandmother at all and only have a very hazy recollection of my Grandfather, which must have been at the time of my Grandmother's death. He gave me some pots and pans to play with in a heap of clean sawdust in one of the outhouses at Brogdale Farm, Leeds, near Maidstone

Starting school

I remember my first day at school very clearly in January 1931. There were huge fires in the classrooms and cloakroom where we hung up our coats. I cried when my Mum left me and went home with my brother and sister, but I was OK in class and settled down to learn at a desk near the fire, which I liked, and next to another desk where a boy called Stanley Curley sat. He was the son of the head gardener of Fox Hill House, Keston, where my Dad worked, and he had learning difficulties. He kept standing on his desk to look out of the windows (which were high up) to see whether his Mum was waiting for him.

My teacher was called Miss Dearsly and she was lovely and I liked her very much. There were four teachers in our Church of England School at Keston. I can only remember three of the teachers who were there at that time, Miss Dearsly for infants, Miss Pavey for class two. The name of the teacher for class three escapes me. Mr Hawkins, the Headteacher, for class four.

All pupils who wanted it could have a third of a pint of milk to drink at morning playtime, this cost ½d a bottle. I did not have it because I did not like milk and could never drink whole milk anyway. I still cannot drink it even now, it always has to be half milk and half water. During the winter, the bottles were stood by the fire guards round the fires to warm up, and sometimes it got so hot it bubbled out of the top of the bottles.

    The milk was always delivered by a horse-drawn milk float, and one day in winter it was very snowy and icy, and the poor horse slipped over outside the school door and tipped the milk float over, spilling the milk. The harness had to be un-hitched from the float to get him back onto his feet, and all the big boys helped to right the float and clear up the mess.

Before I moved out of the infant class, Miss Dearsley left and Miss Jarvis came to teach us, and although she was very different I liked her. She was the typical 1930's fashion woman, very thin and flat, bobbed hair and drop-waisted dresses. At playtime, she smoked cigarettes in long holders. After I left school to go to the School of Craft and Industrial Design in Bromley, I used to help her with teaching her class during my long college holidays. She could not pay me, but always insisted on giving me lovely presents.

    Miss Pavey was another lovely teacher, and during my time in her class I was ill and missed school for a whole year.

She used to send me flowers and little delicacies to tempt my appetite. It was while I was in her class that I started learning to play the piano and compose music. I also won two prizes for Nature Study. I visited and kept in touch with Miss Pavey until she died in the late 1950's.

On Ascension Day, Ash Wednesday, the whole school walked in a crocodile to the Parish Church for a service, and then the afternoon was a holiday.

In May we celebrated Empire Day, when all the boys wore their best suits and the girls wore white dresses and hair ribbons. The previous day, the big boys had marked out a large square with trowels and spades on the common, which was our school playground. In the morning, the boys and the Headmaster would haul the piano into the middle of the square, and also erect a pole with a Union Jack at the top. Later that morning, the whole school would march out there and take our places round the square, where we would sing a hymn, pray and listen to an address from the Headmaster.

Various prizes would be given out. One year, I won a book for making a study of a robin and a beech tree for a whole year. Then we would all march round and salute the flag, sing another hymn and then go home for lunch. The afternoon was a holiday.

Finding my feet

When I was about nine years old, Mr Hawkins retired and Mr Godden took his place. He was much stricter on discipline, and had a wonderful tenor voice. When it was snowy, he often came out and played snowballs with us. About this time, Miss Loader came to teach class three. She was a P.E. fanatic and I was not any good at games or P.E., because I was so small, but got on alright with her when I moved up into her class, because my Mum taught me needlework and I was good at that. Mrs Godden, the headmaster's wife, also taught me how to sew and embroider, which I've loved ever since. Miss Loader had to teach needlework and was not good at it, so I used to teach her how to do it so that she could then teach the class.

All the way through the school, I won the prizes for needlework, many for painting and composition, one for arithmetic, and also one for poetry - learning and reciting 'Ruth' by Thomas Hood. I won several for music, history and geography, and at the end of my last year, I won the Character Prize. The whole of your time in school from 5-14 years was looked at, and it was awarded to the most deserving child. I was bowled over when my name was called out. The prize was a writing case, which I still have.

    Prize giving was held in the village hall, where the whole school, parents and village dignitaries were assembled, and it was a big occasion and we did not know who had won the character prize until your name was called. That day, I was told I had won a place at the Craft School too, to start in January 1940.

We never had school dinners but went home, and Mum used to give us 1d each to take the bus back, but we used to run all the way back to school and give Mum our pennies to help pay for the re-charging of the accumulators for the wireless, which we got in 1935.

During the summer, Mum used to pack us a lovely picnic, which the three of us, Bubs, Betty and I, would take onto the common to sit and eat together. At playtime we used to play Cowboys and Indians and make camps and climb trees and swing on the branches. I used to play a lot of Stoolball which I enjoyed very much, but I hated Netball.

The Headmaster's house was attached to the school and his daughter, Lois, was in my class and was one of my friends. The infants class came out at 3.30pm and the rest of the school at 4pm and so my parents arranged with Mr. Hawkins and his wife that if ever she was not there to meet me, I was to play with Lois at her home and go home with Nellie Bone. She was our next door neighbour's daughter. One day, I thought everyone had gone home without me, and left Lois's garden and started walking home across the Common.

When I got to the bushy part, I was grabbed by my hand by a man and walked down a sideways path and then pushed to the ground and told to stay there while he went to his car. As soon as he was out of sight, I ran like the wind in the opposite direction to the road, and there was my Mum coming to meet me with my brother and Betty in the pram. I can still remember clearly what that man looked like and what he was wearing.

When I was in the top class, Mr Godden's, the Mayor of Bromley had a competition for all the schools in the Bromley area, to paint chrysanthemums. I picked a bunch of double bronze chrysanths from my Dad's garden, took them to school and painted them. There were different classes in the competition for different ages and I won first prize in my class.

I had to go to Bromley to receive the prize from the Mayor. It was a lovely box of paints and brushes which have been well used, and which I still have.

Granny's

I spent a lot of time at my Granny's at Priors Cottage, Keston, where Granny, Grandad and Auntie Dot lived.

I would sleep in Auntie Dot's bedroom, and she would get up early and I would hear her riddle the fire in the kitchen range and push the big kettle across the top to where she had lifted the cover off to boil for tea. In the summer, the bedroom window would be wide open, and I could hear all the country noises, chickens, cows, horses, birds, and the Smithy hammering on his anvil at the Smithy next door. His name was Mr. Irwin.

I used to sit up in bed and compete by singing my favourite songs and hymns at the top of my voice. My Grandparents and Auntie always said they enjoyed it. I wonder if they did! 'Summer Suns are Glowing', 'All Things Bright and Beautiful', 'Loving Shepherd of Thy Sheep', 'Bobby Shafto', 'Strawberry Fair', 'Thro' Tara's Halls', 'The Ash Grove' were some of the things I sang.

Priors Cottage. From left to right are Auntie Kitty, Grandad, Uncle Bill, Granny and Dad

When I was young, Auntie Dot taught me a little song about an engine, and the driver turns the little handle and 'Ifty, Pifty, Shifty, off we go'.

Auntie Lizzy was ladies' maid to Miss Joyce Boosey, whose parents were the music publishers and lived at Knightons, the big house at the top of the school common. She bought Bubs and I a little boat each, and used to take us to the Library Gardens in Bromley to sail them on the lake. Then we would have tea at the coffee shop opposite the entrance in the High Street before going home. She also gave me a pink frilly frock that I treasured, and wore until I could not squeeze myself into it any more.

My lovely Granny (Dad's Mother)

Sundays

On Sundays we would have a special treat. My Dad would bring us a cup of tea in bed with a custard cream biscuit. We used to make the biscuit last as long as we could. When we were old enough, we used to creep downstairs to make tea, and take tea and biscuits to Mum and Dad for them to have in bed.

We got up at 7am and had early Communion before breakfast. We dressed in our Sunday best clothes and after breakfast, Bubs, Betty and I walked down the lane past the Church to Blackness Farm then along Jackass Lane, to see Granny, Grandad and Auntie Dot.

We would walk home again in time for Sunday dinner at 1pm, a roast cooked by Mum. In the afternoon, we went to Children's Church, a service for children in Keston Parish

Church. We would take turns to give the books out, ring the bells and collect the money and do all the chores, and also read the lesson. Mr Brunker was the Organist, and the Vicar, the Curate or Mr. Rogers, the Lay Reader, took the service. We took turns to read the lessons.

The Curate was a young man, who seemed a bit mad, but he had a car, so he was very popular! On Wednesdays, we'd pile into his car and he'd take us to the Youth Club.

After Children's Church, Dad dressed in his Sunday best and would take us for a walk. On the way home, he would buy us one 6d (2½p) vanilla ice cream from the ice cream bicycle man standing at the entrance to Holwood Park, by Holwood Farm on the Downe Road. We would hurry home to cut it into three and have it with our Sunday tea. We would offer Mum and Dad a taste, but they always insisted that we ate it all up. In the evening, we would all go to Evensong at the Church at 6.30pm. Dad was a Sidesman (assistant churchwarden).

We always attended festival services - Easter, Whitsun, Harvest, Armistice and of course Christmas. Armistice was always on the Sunday at the War Memorial, and I was always given a bunch of chrysanths from the garden to lay at the memorial at the end of the service, with all the others who were representing their families.

When I was older, I joined the Church choir and often sang descant and sometimes solo. Now I cannot sing a note, and sometimes long to have a good sing and only a noise comes out, which I find frustrating.

Hayes Common fire

During the summer holidays one year, Hayes Common caught fire and it burned for three days. The whole of the Common was burnt. The people in the cottages near the cross roads were evacuated. It was very exciting for us. Mum used to let us walk to Hayes village each day with Nellie Bone, the 'big girl' who was about thirteen years old, who lived next door. We watched from the green in front of The Greyhound pub, near The Fox Inn, and we came home covered in soot smuts.

Granny's again

During haymaking, I can remember helping Granny and Auntie Dot pack a picnic in white cloths in large baskets, and fill large cans with sweet tea, and carry it out to the fields where Grandad and other people were working. We would sit under a shady tree or hedge, and really enjoy our picnic.

I remember turning the hay with a hay fork for it to dry, and gathering it into heaps for the man to pitch it onto the hay wagon, to be carted away to the farmyard to be made into haystacks for the winter. We children would romp in the hay with Auntie Dot and Uncle Tom sometimes, who were always ready to play with us and were fun.

Auntie Dot would always come with us into the meadow to play with our bats and balls, or any other games we thought of, and when I stayed, she would take me with her to Bromley shopping.

We used to buy groceries at the International Stores and the Home and Colonial Stores, where there were marble counters and scales with brass weights, and large round cheeses to cut on cheese boards with wire cutters. There was sawdust on the floors, which I liked to scuff and slide in, and of course there were lovely smells, and hams and sides of bacon to be sliced on the bacon slicers.

We also went to the Chemist in the Market Square to buy a packet of Bismuth Tablets for Granny for her indigestion. Any haberdashery needed was bought at Dafforns in Widmore Road, nearly opposite the Co-op.

Teatime

When we came home from school, Mum would get tea ready. We usually had it before Dad got home from work. When we were sat round the table with Mum having our tea, she would usually play records and I remember one of our favourites was 'The Ride of the Valkeries' by Wagner. We used to jog up and down on our chairs in time with the music. 'In a Monastery Garden', 'By the Shalimar', 'Donna è Mobile' by Mozart, Schubert's 'Unfinished Symphony', and 'The Laughing Policeman' which had us falling about laughing. We always enjoyed the records.

Later, when Dad was eating his dinner, we would sit and talk to him, and sometimes he would give us a taste or a tit-bit from his plate.

During the winter at dusk, the Muffin Man would come by ringing his bell and carrying his tray of muffins and crumpets on his head. We would buy crumpets, and sit round the fire toasting them on the toasting fork, which I now have on the little corner shelf which the flasks stand on in the kitchen. We would butter them while they were hot, and eat them while we sat round the fire looking for pictures in the fire and watching the shadows round the room. After tea, Mum would light the gaslight and draw the curtains.

Christmas

When we had a lot of snow and ice during the winter, Keston fishponds would freeze over, and when we were little, I can remember my Dad taking Bubs and me in the evening, when it was dark, to the fish ponds to watch people skating. People would come in their cars (only well-off people had cars and skates) and park them on the banks with the headlights left on, directed onto the pond to floodlight it. It was magic to watch these lucky people twirling about on the ice in the light of the cars, and sometimes by moonlight.

I remember shopping in Bromley with Mum one Christmas time, and there were market stalls all round the Market Square. On one stall was a boss-eyed puppet, that dropped its head from side to side and its eyes always went in the opposite direction to its head. The stalls were lit by lanterns and fire torches.

At Christmas time in 1938, Mum took me shopping with her and it was a very memorable occasion for me. She bought me a lovely winter coat with a matching hat. It was blue grey with little flecks of colour in it. The first coat that was bought for me, as mine were hand me downs or home made but they were always nice. We always had new shoes though, never hand me downs.

The run-up to Christmas was always full of secrets, rustling paper and excitement. It was very difficult to get to sleep on Christmas Eve. We would wake very early on Christmas morning and feel for our Christmas stocking, a long black one each. Bubs would come into our room with Betty and me, and by torchlight we would unpack them. There was always an orange in the toe and a sugar mouse. Maybe there would be pencils, crayons and painting books, new hair ribbons, little packets of sweets and an apple, all sorts of small and very welcome gifts. After all this, we would go back to sleep until it was time to wake up.

One Christmas morning, Bubs woke us up and said there was a large mysterious box in his room, which he could not bring into our room and we had better go to his room and help him unwrap it. Very exciting it was too, especially when it turned out to be a railway train with lots of trucks, carriages and lines.

We would all have a jolly breakfast together, and open one or two of our presents. Then all would help with the chores and cooking the dinner, which we liked to finish in time to hear greetings from around the world and the King's speech. After this we would open the rest of our presents and then settle down to games. Ludo, Draughts, Halma, Snakes and Ladders, Whist, Happy Families, Shove Ha'penny, Darts and Bagatelle.

We would set the Christmas tea and sit round the fire to eat it and there was always celery with bread and butter and cheese, mince pies and Christmas cake. After tea, more games until late. When we were older, it was often until 1am.

The Christmas tree was branches of Yew, which Dad brought home. We could not afford to buy one. We put these into a large flowerpot of earth and made absolutely sure that they were firm because we had real candles on it. I still have the holders and some candles. It made a very pretty tree.

On Boxing Day, we went to Granny and Grandad. Auntie Dot and Uncle Bill were there and Auntie Liz and Auntie Kitty. If they did not have to work, Uncle Tom, Auntie Agnes and Robert. After dinner, we would all play more games. We would have tea, and Granny's Christmas cake always had fondant-icing sweets in pretty pastel colours placed on the icing in patterns.

More games until very late and, during the evening, turkey sandwiches and drinks or tea would be handed round. It was a small cottage to have so many people all at once, but our Grandparents loved to have us together for the festival, and our Christmases were always full of fun and laughter.

We would leave Granny in time to walk up Fox Hill to the village, to catch the midnight bus to Downe. We got off at Keston Parish Church. One Boxing night we missed it and, after a few minutes, a car came along and the driver offered us a lift, which we accepted. I was frightened for some reason, and screamed and kicked until we were dropped off outside our house. None of us knew the driver, and I did not feel safe. Betty was a baby so I was about seven years old.

Pantomime and the Santa Claus Grotto

When I was nine or ten years old, Mum took us one Saturday afternoon to see a Pantomime. Auntie Agnes and Robert came with us and we had a lovely afternoon watching 'Old Mother Hubbard' at the Lewisham Hippodrome. I have a very vivid memory of Mother Hubbard and I am fairly sure it was Arthur Askey. If not, it was someone very like him.

On several occasions, we went to Chiesmans in Lewisham to see Father Christmas in his Grotto. He always gave us a present. One year I had a coral necklace that I wore for years. I have given it to Anne (my sister). Another year, I had a necklace of red lucky beans that I used to wear a lot, and still have.

Once, we saw a demonstration of levitation. A lady in a long blue dress was laying flat on a long table, and a man played a penny whistle and she rose into the air, still laying flat as though she was asleep. I still wonder how it was done.

Birthdays

Sunday August 11th was my Mum's birthday, and I used to creep downstairs and into the garden before 7.30am, when Dad left for work, and without being seen. Betty, Bubs and I had a patch of garden each towards the end of our back garden, and I would go to mine and pick a bunch of flowers to give to Mum on her birthday.

At the beginning of the war, we had saved our pocket money to buy Mum a really nice present, and Mum had left to clean the house for two teachers who lived nearby. I dashed off to the village on my bike, and bought a beautiful box of really good chocolates from the Post Office. The box had yellow roses on it.

On another birthday, when things were hard to get during the war, we bought her a wooden tray from the Co-op in Bromley that she rather liked. I still use it now.

We often bought books for Dad's birthday, as he was a great reader and often read aloud to us on winter evenings whilst Mum, Betty and I sewed and knitted. Bubs was usually carving or doing some sort of craft and we were all gathered round the fire, reluctant to leave for bed, because all the other rooms were cold.

May Queen

The May Queen was a big event that we all looked forward to, and it was always held on the first Saturday in May. I cannot ever remember being cold or wet. Once it was dull and cool, and my Mum gave me the baby shawl to pull round my shoulders whilst waiting for things to start. It was a large round one, beautifully knitted in very fine white wool.

The May Queens assembled along a road on Hayes Common, and then processed to Hayes Church, where the London and Merrie England May Queens with their attendants and various other people, including Jack O' The Green, were taking part in a short service.

We all then proceeded back to a large open area on the common, where a maypole had been erected with the

London and Merrie England Queens following at the end. They sat on thrones on a decorated platform at one side of a circle.

The May Queen in 1934. I'm second from the right.

During the afternoon, each Queen, with her train and banner bearers, would walk round the circle to the Merrie and London Queens, curtsey to them and say 'Hail my Lady

Queen of the May' and received a small gift from them. We would then carry on round the circle back to our places, where the rest of our attendants were waiting. There was maypole dancing and music.

Each Realm had its own colours and flower. Ours, Leaves Green, was cowslip yellow and leaf green, and the flower was the cowslip. Keston was red and white, and their flower was white heather.

After the celebrations on Hayes Common, each Queen went home with all of her attendants, and had a tea party.

Sickness

When one of us was sick, we would go into Mum and Dad's bed. Our beds were warm and comfortable, but Mum's bed was special, and we would be nursed back to health with Mum's wonderful nursing and special tender loving care from both parents.

Mum always slept with us and, if my brother was sick, Dad would sleep in his bed. If Betty or I were sick, Dad would sleep on the sofa downstairs. When Dad returned home from work, he would bring us little bunches of grapes, which were expensive and very special.

I had pleurisy and pneumonia, and on both occasions, Mum put hot poultices on my ribs, which I found comforting because they relieved the pain. No antibiotics in those days. I can also remember Mum rubbing goose grease on our chests and backs at bedtime when we had chesty coughs or colds. Mum also used to mix up honey and lemon on a spoon for coughs, and for sore throats, a pinch of yellow sulphur powder on the end of a teaspoon handle, which was placed on our tongues and blown into our throats. It worked! For upset tummies, a teaspoon of brandy in hot water (that had been boiled).

We did have measles and chicken pox, and Bubs and Betty had mumps, but fortunately not diphtheria or scarlet fever because you were taken to an isolation hospital in a fever ambulance. Whilst there, only parents were allowed to make very few visits, and then only see you from the other side of a glass panel.

I remember a girl of about my age, who lived four doors away, being taken to a fever isolation hospital, which was at Bromley Common near the bus garage. Whenever we saw an ambulance, we used to stand on one leg until it was out of sight and recite, "Touch your collar, never swallow, never get the fever".

Dancing

When I was about nine years old, I joined the Co-op Guild, which met once a week at 'The Ramblers Rest Hall', Leaves Green. In July each year, the Co-op had a huge pageant at Wembley Stadium, and ours and several other guilds did Country Dancing. We wore knee length dresses with full skirts. Half of us in dark lavender, the other half in light lavender. Other groups were in dark and light green, dark and light lemon or pink or yellow, all the colours of the rainbow.

The day was always warm and sunny, and thousands of us assembled, and whenever I see footballers coming through the tunnel onto the pitch, I re-live those afternoons when I and my companions streamed through the tunnels to dance round the arena to our places, and then perform our dances to thousands of spectators. Mum, Betty and Bubs were three of them, and I said I would wave to them, but could not see them, just a sea of faces.

Some years, we went to the Crystal Palace and danced on the open-air arena there. In 1939 we danced the Sailors Hornpipe at Redhill, and were mobbed by the crowd.

Once a week, after school, Miss Pavey and Miss Loader took country-dance classes, which I joined when I was about ten. I enjoyed them very much. I have always loved dancing, and still do, and when suitable music comes on the radio, I dance around the house.

When Betty and I were old enough, we went ballroom dancing and Scottish dancing and we loved that. We used to square dance with Charles Chiltern, and do Scottish dancing with Jimmy Shand. Both used to be on the radio. We went to Scottish dance classes at West Wickham with Edith Henney, Pam and Yolande. We danced with Jimmy Shand at the Bloomsbury Ballroom in London. I also went to a Conservative Ball there.

Games and activities

We had lots of oblong wooden bricks all the same size, and we used to stand them all on end in various lines, sometimes curvy, sometimes straight. Then we would tap the first one, which would tap the next and the next until they had all fallen down. We used to call this game 'Drowndrons', our own name for it. We also played Housey Housey which is now called Bingo.

Me as Alice in Wonderland

I belonged to the Co-op Guild, and one year we did 'Alice Through The Looking Glass', and I was Alice. I had long hair and the colouring of Alice in the books, and Mum made the perfect outfit. I ended up looking exactly like Alice in the picture books, right down to my white socks and black shoes.

I joined the Brownies for a short while but it was not really my scene, and after a short while I left.

Bubs belonged to the Cubs and Scouts, and they used to put on shows at the Village Hall. Once he was a 'Nigger Minstrel' (which was accepted in those days), and came onto the stage with white hands, black feet and face, with large white lips. He was dressed in striped pyjamas, carrying a Banjo which he 'played', and sang 'Swanee River'.

Outings

We used to go on outings with various groups - The Co-op Guild, Mother's Union, Busman's outing and a Mother's Group from the Chapel on Leaves Green.

The Co-op chartered a train that used to take us with our Mothers to Littlehampton, which was fun. We used to take our picnic lunch and have it on the sands or wherever, and then meet up at a hall where we always had a lovely tea.

The Busman's outing was similar, but we always went to Sheerness by coach, and each child was given a bag of crisps to eat on the way or with our picnic lunch. There was a funfair near the beach, and once we went on the Bumper Cars, that we really enjoyed. Huge fun bumping into each other! We all met up for tea at a large hall, before boarding the coach for the return journey home.

At the beach, Betty, me and Bubs, from left to right

I remember clearly the Mother's Group went to Hastings when I was about seven years old. We went by coach through Biggin Hill, and as we were passing along the top of Westerham Hill, on the left there was a lovely meadow covered in white daisies wafting in the breeze. It was beautiful. I have passed this hundreds of times since and never again seen it like that. Also on the Tonbridge side of Sevenoaks, I remember Mum pointing out to us Knole House, and telling us about it.

This was the first time I saw the sea, and being on the beach watching it and playing and paddling in it, and a few days later visiting Granny and telling her all about my day. She was a lovely Granny.

We had a day out at the Crystal Palace with the Co-op Guild. It was a fantastic place. There was a little funfair there, and I remember seeing my Mum come down the Helter Skelter. Mum was always fun. We also went to Maidstone Zoo once, and that was exciting and interesting.

During the summer, Mum and Dad used to take us out walking and picnics, usually on a Sunday afternoon in Holwood Park. Also on the Keston Common around the ponds. We always took bats and balls for games. Mum and Dad always played with us. In the school holidays, Mum would make us a picnic, and we would go to the fields opposite our home and build a camp with our school friends, where we would play and have our picnic.

Wartime

War breaks out

I was almost 14 when the Second World War broke out. We knew there was a war coming, talking about it, we knew it would involve everybody and we knew that things would be rough because we just sensed that there would be all this stuff flying around. The war was in the foreground all the time, because you were short of food.

At the end of August 1939, Dad and Bubs stayed with Uncle Ted and Auntie Alice at East Farleigh near Maidstone for a week's holiday. It was lovely sunny summer weather but the news was bad. Bubs and Dad returned home on Saturday 2nd September and war was declared on Sunday 3rd. A day I remember very clearly, we listened to Mr Chamberlain on the wireless at 11am. There was an air raid warning, Mum cooked the Sunday roast dinner and Dad did the gardening. After dinner, Bubs, Betty and I got ready for Children's Church. We all had Sunday tea about 5pm and then we went to Evensong at 6.30pm. Dad then watered the garden and Mum put the washing to soak ready for tomorrow and we children helped with the chores, so that we all sat down together until bedtime.

When we returned to school, we only went for half of each day, because the air raid shelters were not finished. Mum fitted us all out with new clothes, hoping they would fit and last a long time.

I remember one thing about this time very clearly. At the beginning of term I had to go to Bromley Art School for my oral examination, and I walked out the front garden which sloped up to the road and I was walking along the hedge at the top, and Bubs and Betty were standing at the door waving to me. Mum wasn't there because she had to go to work, and Dad was working, so it was just my brother and sister there, and Gracie Fields was singing "Wish me luck as you wave me goodbye" on the radio. So I was looking over the top of the hedge, waving back and singing, "Wish me luck as you wave me goodbye", I don't know what it sounded like, and they were at the door waving to me and singing, "We wish you luck as we wave you goodbye" as I went up the road to get on the bus.

School of Craft and Industrial Design

I passed my exams and started at the School of Craft and Industrial Design in Bromley, in January 1940. I loved every minute of it. The school was next door to Bromley Art School, and the same teachers taught in both schools, and we spent quite a lot of our time in the Art School.

There were six of us to a teacher, and we had to design everything we made - embroideries, machine and hand dressmaking, needlework and painting. We also had general education at the commercial school and we had Miss Penwell to teach us ballroom dancing and P.E. in the hall behind our school, and tennis on the courts at Hayes during the summer. We always danced to the music of Victor Sylvester.

During the air raids, which were many, we took work into the air raid shelter that was situated underneath the school garden and worked as best we could.

We had long summer holidays and I used to help Miss Jarvis, the infant teacher at Keston, with her class.

Bubs left school at the age of 14 and went to work with Dad at the Council Gardens in Hayes. He was always kind and generous and, until I left the craft school and started earning, he gave me 2½d (6p), which was worth a lot more than it is now.

Food and everything was short and there were always queues. One day, I heard that there were biscuits in Woolworths, and I dashed down there and managed to buy a bag of cream crackers before running for my bus home. I slipped when boarding it, and hit my chest on the corner of the platform, so Mum had a bag of crumbs and biscuits.

At Craft School we all had school dinners, which were jolly good. You could tell the day of the week by what you were eating, and Friday was my favourite. Hot cheese pastry with cooked tomatoes, potatoes and peas, followed by fruit and custard.

Getting by

Food wasn't rationed then, but it was hard to get. You had to run around and somebody would say "Oh, the butcher down there's got some meat", and everybody would rush down there. It was far worse than when it was rationed, because then you knew how much you were going to get, and you queued up at the shop and you got your ration.

When it was short, you could stand there, hoping to get something, and you never knew how long you were going to be and whether there would be anything when you got to the front. You couldn't just go into a shop and say I'll have this, that and the other, it wasn't there. Mum had to run around all day and stand and queue and get whatever she could - butter and bread and meat. She was doing her best, it was amazing the amount she stretched it.

I used to help Mum with the shopping, and spent many hours queuing at Kennedy's for sausages or anything else that might be going. That shop was still in Bromley in 2000, still selling sausages and their famous pies.

My Dad was a gardener, and grew lots of vegetables at home. We used to work with him, we watched how he did it and we used to sow seeds and plant vegetables. He had a rough time in the First World War and gardening was the best occupation he could have had, it's a very healing thing to do, you're growing things that are alive and coming up, it really is, and it helped a lot that we'd got a garden.

My brother and sister and I all had a patch where we grew seeds and plants for the kitchen and flowers to pick to make life worth living. I just grew anything that I could make grow, and my Dad would pick a bunch of flowers and bring them in for my Mum and hand them to her, because you couldn't go out and buy flowers. Anyway, the ones from the garden were much better.

Avoiding evacuation

At the start of the war, Mum and Dad arranged for us to be evacuated, to stay with our Uncle Harry, Mum's cousin in Calgary, Canada.

Auntie Liz helped Mum get all our clothes labelled and packed, but the day before we were supposed to be going, while my parents were downstairs by the fire, my brother, sister and I went to my room and we had a meeting and we said "we are NOT going to Canada, we are not going anywhere". After the meeting, we came downstairs, my Mum and Dad were sitting by the fire, and we went into the room and sat in front of them and said, looking at them, "we are NOT going to Canada, if there is going to be a war we will see it through together here with you", and we did. There was no way we were going anywhere.

A lot of children were evacuated and a lot of children died because the Germans torpedoed the boat that they were on, because that was the boat we should have been on, the SS City of Benares. We never thought about sailing over the sea though, that was a big adventure, we just did not want to go.

The Anderson shelter

When we got home from work or school, Mum would have a meal for us and we would sit and have that. Sometimes at night, we would have our tea and Mum would see us to bed quite early sometimes, to get some sleep before all the planes and bombs began.

Like many homes, we had an Anderson shelter at the end of the garden. We'd put our old clothes on and go down the Anderson shelter in the evening. We had one of those hurricane lights, they were wonderful because they were safe. You could light the lamp and you could walk around with it, it was safe because it was enclosed in the glass. You could stand it anywhere, on the table so that you could write or sew or knit.

We would all sit round at night knitting, and we were knitting for the seamen because we could get the wool, very thick, oily wool. It wasn't very nice to handle but we used to make long stockings for the seamen to have on in their boats at sea because they were travelling up north, near the North Pole, coming down into the port there, to get into Russia.

Fund raising

Churchill used to live at Chartwell and used to go past my house. Lady Churchill did a lot of work for the Russian Red Cross during the war, for the men in Russia. So I joined that and raised money for it by making all sorts of things in the needlework line and then selling them.

I would have Christmas sales, making soft toys because you couldn't buy toys for children, and they were soft toys for the little ones, so I made lots of those, and teddy bears. And I'd make dolls, and dress them so that they could unbutton them and take their clothes off properly, which not many dolls did, the clothes were always stuck on the dolls somehow. We were very busy at Christmas time, and sat up till 1am and 2am sometimes to finish them in time. We also knitted with wool we collected from the headquarters in Wigmore Street, London.

Betty and I also joined the Anglo-Soviet Youth Friendship Alliance, and exchanged letters with pen friends in Russia. Mine was called Shura Tchakasky from Tbilisi in Georgia. I also received handwritten and signed letters from Lady Churchill, thanking us for the money raised for the Russian Red Cross. Sadly, all of these letters have disappeared.

Betty and I were invited to an Anglo-Soviet Youth Friendship Alliance afternoon reception in Northumberland Avenue in London and took the afternoon off. I dressed in my best clothes and went. Betty could not come so Marjory took her place. We all had to wear proper evening dresses, so I made my own.

We walked downstairs, and were met by footmen, dressed in powder blue 17th century costumes and powdered wigs, that announced us. We were greeted by Sir Stafford and Lady Cripps, and the Russian Ambassador, Mr. Vishinksky (later head of the KGB). They shook our hands and welcomed us. There was a wonderful buffet, lots of silver and crystal, a dazzling site in wartime, and entertainment by the pianist Moura Lympany. I listened to her in many concerts in later years.

Waiting for the planes to return

We lived very close to the aerodrome and could see the planes on the end of the runway, and we used to watch them go out when we heard the engines warming up for another battle.

We had a better view from the road, which sloped up a bit from the house, so we used to go out into the front garden and stand up on the road and watch them take off. We'd walk up to the pavement, and quite often we'd cross the road into the field leading up to the end of the runway where they took off and landed.

We'd count them, then we'd wait to see how many came back. We would keep waiting and waiting because sometimes there was one missing, hadn't arrived home, and we'd keep waiting as long as we possibly could for it to come back. Sometimes they didn't, and we felt very sad because we were wondering what had happened to the pilot, whether he'd come down in the sea, or whether it'd caught fire when it landed, because that happened sometimes, and we would see it at Biggin Hill when that happened. It would come down onto the runway and suddenly it would burst into flames and we just ran as close as we could get, hoping the pilot was alright. Sometimes he was and sometimes he wasn't, and then we felt very sad. It was awful, and I know I used to cry a lot.

Open House

The pilots were so young, they were just boys, some of them just 19 years old probably, and there were lots of foreign ones. The people all round the aerodrome used to have what they called Open House, where the pilots could come along, knock on the door, and we would let them in and give them cups of tea and, if it was evening, we'd sit round the fire and talk.

They were a long way from home and they never went into a house because they were in barracks all the time, and they were fighting, and they used to help wash up and make the tea and have a bit of time in the home with the family round the fire.

Mum was very generous and she used to invite people in and cook and make cookies and things that they could have with their cups of tea and coffee. I used to sit and talk to the pilots with my sister and brother, push the table back to the wall and we'd all sit round the fire, because the weather was cold, and just talk. There were quite a few from Poland, they could speak in broken English (we couldn't speak Polish, of course), and we would talk slowly to them. They were glad to be friends with people like the English who were trying to release their country and free it up again.

I remember one pilot called Jan, who was Polish. He used to come home and sit by the fire in the evening, food was short but Mum always used to find something. Sometimes we would go off to the pictures, just friends going out to the pictures, relief from all the other stuff that was happening.

There was nothing serious about it, maybe there was from his side but I wasn't really interested, no way was I thinking about marrying a foreigner and leaving England. I wouldn't live anywhere else but England or the British Isles. A lot of girls did, a lot of them stayed over here and married English girls, but it didn't appeal to me at all.

Jan, my Polish pilot friend

I think Jan was quite keen, I think he had the idea he wanted to marry me, I seemed to feel that from him sometimes, but no, I was English and I was staying in England.

The Leaves Green Dornier

There was no air raid warning. It was a misty Sunday morning and Betty and I were indoors helping Mum with Sunday dinner, Bubs was helping Dad in the garden, when we heard a plane flying very low, and by the sound of the engine it was a German.

The plane (a Dornier 17, attacked while bombing Biggin Hill and Kenley) came across from Holwood House, over Downe Road, and behind the council houses. We could see that it was struggling to land, and it needed to get its wheels down. I can't remember whether they were down or not, I know they were struggling to get it down.

We all dashed into our air raid shelter when it dropped a bomb on the Rectory next to Keston Parish Church. It went into the cellar and blew the foundations out, but the house still stood. There was a terrible noise, as though someone was dragging a Dutch Barn across the fields, which went on and on. Then there was total silence.

We came out of our shelter and stood at the front gate, looking across the fields at this huge cloud of black smoke, and gradually more people clambered out of their shelters. The plane had gone across the first field, which went up to the aerodrome on the other side of the road from our house, up the bank, through the hedge, and half way across the second field. It crashed, on fire, facing the aerodrome, approximately 700 yards from the boundary.

We ran across the fields to capture the pilot - we thought it would be great if we could capture one of the enemy! We ran up to the wreckage, which was on fire, and two crew had came out, and we were going to capture them, but the men from the aerodrome had run down there and they took over. We were so disappointed!

The crew were standing about 50 yards from the burning plane, looking very dejected. The hands and face of the pilot (Rudolph Lamberty) were burnt. Somebody undid his flying jacket and took out a packet of English Players cigarettes which he had bought in the Channel Islands, which were under German occupation. Somebody lit one for him and gave it to him.

The Air Force Police came across the fields in a lorry and picked them up and took them to the aerodrome First Aid Post, and then to Farnborough Hospital.

The rear gunner parachuted into the field at the back of our houses and scrambled down the bank into Blackness Lane to a pair of cottages. He went to the air-raid shelter which was occupied by Mrs. Friend. He gave her quite a shock when he appeared at the entrance. The RAF police collected him later, and took him to join his colleagues at Farnborough Hospital.

Guards from the Army arrived to guard the wreckage of the plane. They were forgotten by their mates at camp, and were left without any supplies of food, water or equipment, apart from rifles. They had a small tent which they put up in the hedgerow for camouflage. The local population supplied cans of tea and sandwiches until rations arrived for them.

Later in the day, the Germans tried to bomb the plane to destroy any specialist equipment which may have been useful to us. The RAF removed all equipment from it.

Being bombed

There were lots of bombing raids around us, and they didn't care where they dropped their bombs, whether it was on a school or anything, because schools did get bombed and children died. The house on the end of my row did get bombed. I heard it and the next morning, Violet, a school friend of mine, said her home had gone but they were alright.

Sometimes, at school in the morning, because we all had assembly, the headmaster would say "Now, this morning, we won't be seeing Tony and Kenneth any more, they were hit by a bomb last night, or shrapnel from a bomb, and they died". I can remember that clearly because we were all chattering away, and quite suddenly everyone became silent and we were all very sad.

Opposite the houses where we lived, a common sloped up towards the airfield and between our home and the top of the common there's a piece of path going along a bank and the bank sloped down and there was a ditch at the bottom. We were running up the bank to school, and there was an air raid, and we were running up towards the runway end of the aerodrome, up on the ridge at the top, and I seem to remember a huge explosion up there and we were quite close to it, but we were all right.

We could hear all the shrapnel hitting things and we just laid flat on the ground, but of course we should have done that earlier, not after it exploded. No one was seriously hurt, fortunately. I always thought shrapnel would be a cold lump of metal but it isn't, it's a red hot piece of metal that comes out and flies everywhere, and of course it can injure you.

It wasn't just the bombs that were noisy, the dogfights were noisy, carrying on over our heads, and we could also hear the sound of shrapnel hitting things. There were also peaceful moments too. I remember one evening listening to the sound of a cuckoo along the valley outside my window, singing as if it were happy, in the peace of the evening, after the day's bombing had stopped.

Once, a bus went into a tree because of a bomb. As the road went down to Trinity Church, the road at the bottom crossed, going to Bromley one way and to Keston and Biggin Hill the other way, and a tree had gone down, and there was a ditch across there, and we ran across this wide grass verge and rolled down the ditch into it, and sheltered there, and we were alright.

    The ditch was dry, and the grass was clean, dogs and things didn't get round there, fortunately, which was just as well, as I don't what know sort of state we'd have been in if it wasn't. When the raid had cleared and we felt it was safe, we came out and got on the bus and I finally got to Bromley, walked along Southlands Road to the School of Craft and Industrial Design.

I was on the bus travelling to school one morning, and we were nearly at Trinity Church, Bromley Common, when a 'Gerry' plane came over firing its guns. The bus came to an abrupt halt and we all leapt off into the ditch where we sheltered until it disappeared. We finally reached Bromley Market Square, where I alighted from the bus to walk along Widmore Road to school, when bombs started falling and Ack-Ack guns were firing. I dived into the cellar in Dafforns haberdashery shop, and stayed there until the 'all clear' sounded.

Another time, the sirens had sounded, and Betty, Bubs and I were walking along our road a few yards from our gate when planes came over very low, the pilots waved to us. A few seconds later, they dropped bombs on Biggin Hill aerodrome and we scooted to shelter at the bottom of our garden. Betty fell over and grazed her hand quite badly and there was a first aid kit in the shelter, so I was able to clean it up and dress it for her.

We were very worried about Mum because she was cycling to Jail Lane, Biggin Hill, to pay a bill. It turned out that she'd gone via Downe rather than down the main road past the aerodrome, I can't remember why she went that way, but it was a good job she did. The road past the aerodrome was closed, I expect.

Capturing the enemy

A German pilot came down on a parachute into the field behind our houses, and my sister and I ran across to capture him in the field. He came down during the day, early afternoon, jumped out of his plane, which also crashed down there. My sister and I arrived in front of all the men running over, he was just a young boy and was terrified. We'd picked up pitchforks and things that were in the garden as weapons, and he was standing there with his hands up.

We said "Hello, come on, we'll give you a cup of tea" and took him indoors to Mum, and she found some more tea, how on earth she stretched that tea ration I don't know, but it used to go a long way, and we gave him a cup of tea. He came round and we talked to him, as much as we could, talking English, but we got on, then two airman came from the aerodrome and took him up there to the prison, I hope they looked after him and were kind.

I never knew his name or what happened to him, I would like to have known what he did in the end and where he is, I'd love to meet him, see how he's got on in life. I sometimes think about it, I'm sad that I've never been able to do it.

Exploring crash sites

We were quite free to wander round crash sites, the boys used to collect things and bring them into school, all sorts of things, sometimes it was explosive, and they'd been picking it up and running around with it, and put it on the desk.

The headmaster used to say "Take that out to the middle of the common, and make sure you know where it is, so that we can know". Oh dear! The girls didn't seem to do it, it was the boys that were interested in the metal and the shapes, as far as we girls were concerned it was a bit of metal.

We would go and see the sites where planes or bombs came down. There'd be a hole there, bits of metal lying around. Surprisingly, the bomb holes didn't seem very big to me, I thought they'd be great big holes where the bomb had blown it out. If they hit a house, that was it.

I can remember very clearly coming out of our back door, and I could hear glass at the other end of the road shattering, and that was where the windows were blown out. It might have been a plane or a bomb hitting the ground, or something hitting a greenhouse.

Going out in wartime

One Saturday afternoon, Mum, Betty and I decided to give ourselves a treat. It was a pleasant early winter day, and we took the bus to Bromley and another to the cinema in Downham. On the way, Mum, bought a china jug that she needed. The 'Four Feathers' was showing, which we had been hoping to see for a while, and we enjoyed it. We came out of the cinema about 5pm.

It was dark as expected, because of the blackout precautions, but there was also a 'pea-souper' fog, and we could not see our hand held out in front of us, it was so thick. We had to walk home. We had only walked for a very short while when we were stumbling around in somebody's garden, lost.

We got back onto the path and after a while we were near The Swan pub and the Odeon Cinema at Bromley North. Walking by a brick wall, which we could not see, but heard Mum's jug touching it as she walked by, we held each other's hands and looped arms while in the fog because we might have lost each other.

By the time we reached Hayes Lane, we decided to walk in the middle of the road from one cat's eye to the next. We got along a little better, but road junctions were another problem, so when we reached Hayes village we returned to the paths. We reached Hayes Common and there was an air raid. We could hear the planes but kept walking. The enemy could not see us. When we reached home about 10pm it was a beautiful clear moonlight night. Dad was so worried and so pleased see us.

Summer holiday

One August, it must have been 1943, Mum came with us to Paddington Station in London and saw us onto the train for Worcester, where we were going to stay with Auntie Agnes and Uncle Tom (Dad's brother) and Robert for three weeks. They lived at Wychbold, where Uncle worked on the farm, and we had a lovely time.

Auntie and Uncle took us to Malvern and we climbed to the top of one of the hills. We also went to Worcester, and walked by the river and climbed the Cathedral tower.

We went into the harvest fields, and stacked the shucks of corn. Quite a scratchy job.

I remember knitting Mum a jumper in a lovely lavender shade, which suited her and she wore it for years. We must have spared some of our precious coupons for wool. We worried about Mum and Dad, and felt sad that they could not be with us.

One sunny evening, we were walking the meadows and there were hundreds of rabbits feeding. As soon as we appeared, they stopped and were very still, and when we stayed still and quiet they all hopped about and started feeding.

We were not far from Droitwich and there were salt courses. You could tell where they ran by the dead and dying trees.

Starting work

In 1943, after three years at the Craft and Industrial Design School, I started worked in London, as a court dress maker for the House of Worth in Mount Street in the West End of London, near Berkeley Square.

I left home on the 7am bus and caught the workman's train at 7.30am from Bromley South to Victoria. The trains morning and evening were always packed.

There were air raids, and the travelling was very dangerous, although I was never worried about getting shot or injured, but at being thrown onto the electric line and being electrocuted. Once, we were on the train near Sydenham and there was a raid going on, and it appeared to me that the driver was trying to get to a tunnel and go in there.

The train stayed there for quite a while, and I was sitting there thinking that if that plane dropped a bomb at the entrance to the tunnel we won't be able to get out. I didn't say anything about that to anybody, but we just sat there and talked until we could move on, and we got to London and we came out of the train at Victoria Station, and then I had to walk across London to Berkeley Square.

Our workroom was at the top of the building, and to get to it we went up an outside iron fire escape. We worked from 8.30am until 5.30pm with half an hour for lunch, which we ate at the bottom of the fire escape. The loos were across a landing outside the workroom, and the Manager's office was out there, and if he thought you went to the loo too often, he would tell you off. I earned 27/6d a week (£1.37). My weekly train fare was 10/- (50p). This was a good job, and I had to have first class City and Guilds Certificates for dressmaking and design to work there.

I came out of the work room onto the roof once, when there was an air raid, and was looking towards London Bridge where the raid was going on further down the river, and you could see the planes over there. I was just watching them and saw something come down from a plane and explode, and things were blowing up and people were hurt and killed sometimes.

Anyway, sirens went off and I thought 'right, I'm going to get home', so I walked across to Victoria Station and got back to Bromley and got the bus out to Keston, and it was such a relief. I came off the bus at the top of the road and looked down the road, and I could see our row of houses and it was alright, they were there.

Madame Isobel

After a while, I moved along the street to Madame Isobel's (a famous dress designer) near Bond Street. She paid me 35/- (£1.75) and our workroom was at the opposite end to Worth's - in the basement - but the hours were the same.

Sometimes another girl l and I would dash out to Lyons teashop nearby in Bond Street, opposite Fenwick's, and have a Lancashire Hot Pot for lunch, it was delicious.

One day we popped into Fenwicks and had a special of theirs, coffee and tea mixed. We thought it was delicious and we were sitting in the posh shop. The height of luxury! One day we stood in Bond Street looking up to the sky, pretending to watch a plane that could have been German. After a few minutes we looked down and everyone in the street was looking for it while we walked back to work.

London was full of service men and women from all over the world, and when we ate in Lyons, the Yanks would be there, eating strange combinations of food, like bacon with marmalade spread on it. They were a scruffy lot too. We also saw lots of Royalty from everywhere. They had fled from Europe to escape the Germans and Italians.

Bubs was in the army, driving in the RASC (Royal Army Service Corps). There was a big gap in our family, especially Christmas 1944 when he could not get leave. We did have Uncle Harry, Mum's second cousin from Calgary, Canada, who was stationed in London in the Canadian Army.

That Christmas Eve, we had Uncle Harry, our Curate and two Polish airmen join us at the table for supper. We shared a food parcel that Auntie Anne, Uncle Harry's wife had sent him from Canada. Three things I remember from the parcel were whole tinned chicken, a rich fruit cake and a box of roasted nuts. There were eight of us, and we each savoured our portions and made them last as long as possible.

One afternoon, I was called to the labour exchange and directed to work in Farnborough Engineering works. When I told Madame Isobel, she went mad and got me six months deferment. By that time I would be old enough to join up so I volunteered for the ATS (Auxiliary Territorial Service, the women's branch of the British Army), who were asking for people. The week before I had to report to the training unit, I told Madame, and she went absolutely berserk.

On April 1st 1945, my dear Granny died and her funeral was on April 5th. The scent of daffodils and narcissi always remind me of that day. There were many wreaths and all were spring flowers. Tomorrow I was going to the barracks at Leicester to start training in the ATS, and so after Granny's funeral I had to finish my preparations and pack. That evening I could not stop crying. It must have been awful for my poor Mum and Dad.

Joining the ATS

I joined The West Kent Regiment, nicknamed The Buffs, in Maidstone. It was the same regiment my Father was in during the First World War. I told my Mum, and she was not so happy, of course.

I ended up doing needle work in the ATS, having done dress making for Worth's and Madame Isobel, sometimes the uniforms needed altering, you couldn't have a shabby lot of people walking around in clothes with sleeves that were too long, and turnings needed to go up on the trousers, and odd things like that.

April 6th 1945, the day I started, was a lovely spring day and I said goodbye to Dad who went to work at 7.30am. Mum wanted to come to London but I said 'no', only as far as Bromley South Station, where I was to meet Marjorie Rye, also an ex-Craft School student who had also worked at Madame Isobel's, and joined up with me.

Mum always looked nice, and this morning she wore her pretty brown wool suit with a flowery blouse that went with it, and her brown leather court shoes. I said goodbye to Mum on the platform as the train came in, and Marjorie and I climbed in and we were off on our adventure. I was so glad that Marjorie's Mum was there, so they were company for each other.

We were met at the station in Leicester, and taken in three-ton lorries to Wigston Barracks. Our room was a long hut with about forty wooden camp beds in it, and an ablutions room at the end. Beside each bed was a small metal wardrobe and locker. The beds were about a foot high, and there were three hard square straw biscuits on each, which slid about on a shiny board. During the night they parted, and I used to wake up with my head over the end and my bottom on the board.

One sunny morning, while on the parade ground, I thought that this was much better than sitting in a basement workroom, sewing for rich women. One morning we donned our gas masks and went into a gas chamber to test them. All of the gas masks seemed to be OK and we did not suffer any ill effects.

The end of war

While training at Leicester, VE Day (Victory in Europe) was announced on 8th May 1945. They said "Well, the afternoon's free, you can go and do what you like", so Marjorie and I went into Leicester and had tea and wandered around, went to the pictures and saw 'Meet Me in St. Louis', and it was great, but we were shocked and appalled by the newsreels in the cinema about Belsen, a concentration camp that had just been discovered. We were so relieved that the European war was over, now we had to beat the Japanese.

Afterwards, we had some supper, and went back to barracks again, and it was all a bit flat because there was nothing to do and nowhere for us to go, and we just felt a bit flat. We felt there should be singing and dancing and all that, but there was nothing, no singing or dancing in the streets.

At the end of our one month's training, Marjorie and I, with everyone else on the same course, went home on 72 hours leave. It was good to be back home again, and in my own bed.

The months after VE Day, we kept being posted to different bases, where it was needed for our job, we seemed to go all round the country. As we got to each place, they were celebrating, so we joined in those celebrations, spent a lot of time marching in victory parades, and then we got posted to another one, and another one.

After the War

Warrington

We were posted to Peninsula Barracks, Warrington, which was ancient and filthy. There was a tannery on one side of the Barracks and a wire factory on the other, and everything was covered in a thick layer of grime and soot smuts. Once again, we were in a hut with forty four girls, some in two-tier bunks and some had iron beds. We were lucky to be in the beds.

There were six washbasins and loos, and two baths, so there was a rush in the mornings. After a few days of scrubbing out a hut, Marjorie and I worked in the tailor's shop, where we met Peck. We used to spend our weekends in Chester at the YWCA, which was sparsely furnished but clean, and we had a lovely city to explore.

One windy evening, the R.S.M. (Regimental Sergeant Major) had us out on the square to practice drill. I put my hat on as securely as I could and hoped it would not blow off, and it did when we were marching and not 'at ease', so I could not pull it on, and it blew right to the other side of the square. She brought us to a halt and marched away, came to a halt, retrieved my hat, about turned and marched back. She was a very mannish person, and looked so comical that we all had the giggles that we had to suppress. She plonked my hat on my head, about turned and marched back. All this, and I could not move until she gave the next command, and even then could not touch my hat, just carry on marching. Oh, how we laughed when dismissed!

One very wet Sunday afternoon, several of us were lying on our beds, whiling away the time. Someone had found an old wind-up gramophone and we had one record, which we played over and over again. It was called 'Beautiful Dreamer', I don't remember who was singing it though. Marjorie, Peck and I had some of Mum's ginger cake. Mum used to send me food parcels and her ginger cake was scrumptious. How Mum did this on the rations she had, I will never know.

We had a lovely black girl in our hut, she slept in the bed opposite me, and we called her 'Snowy'. She was a really nice girl and Peck and I loved her. Her home was in Liverpool.

Sometimes, two of us were on duty all night in the guardroom and had to open the gate to let people in and out. The place was crawling with cockroaches that came out in the night.

After a few weeks, the three of us were sent to Chester where we lived in a castle, a round tower with slits for windows that looked onto a little dark, dank yard. After a couple of days we were sent on ten days leave because the work had not arrived. Mum and Dad were so surprised to see me unexpectedly that they thought I was absent without leave, until they saw my pass and warrant.

My next posting was to Shrewsbury, and Peck, Marjorie and I travelled together, and I can remember walking from the station to the barracks and dragging my kit bag through the streets in the hope that when the Quartermaster saw the wear and tear that it had he would change it for a grip, and he did. Hooray!

Next morning we reported to the tailors shop, and found a soldier there from the Green Howards, who had been told to clean and oil the machines so that they were ready for us to use.

He had oiled them with rifle oil he said. It was thick stuff and we could not move them, and it took us ages to sort them out.

There were terrible floods while we were there. The river broke its banks and the town and surrounding area was flooded. Near the river, it was racing by, sweeping along trees, cattle and sheds, one full of chickens. All sorts of things were swept away, if it got into a whirlpool it was sucked in and down. It was really terrifying, and did a lot of damage.

Congleton

As the floods were going down, we were posted to Congleton, to three Irish regiments, Inniskillings, Irish Fusiliers, and the London Irish. There were only twenty four ATS girls, and we were billeted with families around the town. Marjorie was in a rotten billet, but Peck and I had good ones.

I was billeted with an elderly couple, Mr and Mrs Cotterill, who lived near the station. They were lovely people, and so kind to me. They were paid 1/9d (about 9p) a week for me to sleep in their spare bedroom. All my meals were in the mess, but they often fed me.

ATS girls marching briskly along, me on the right

Congleton was full of silk mills, that were commandeered by the Army for barrack rooms for the men, and for the Mess, cookhouse and workshops. Every morning, a jeep would come and take us to the Mess for breakfast. There were not any doors on it and you had to hang on tight, or else you would be flung out on the bend down the hill. After breakfast, we walked to another mill to the tailor's shop where we worked from 9am to 5pm, with one hour at 12.30 for dinner. We used to brew up for tea and coffee in the workshop.

After tea at 5pm, we would walk back to our billets, or maybe go to the pictures first, then walk back. One Saturday, we booked the dearest seats in the little cinema 1/6d (7½p) to see 'Harvest Moon', which we enjoyed. When we came out it was almost dark with a huge harvest moon in the sky, and we linked arms and walked back to our billets, singing the song 'Harvest Moon'.

At weekends we used to walk miles along the canal to Mow Cop, and out to Moreton Old Hall and all over the place. I did quite a lot of sketching.

During our posting in Congleton, we all took part in the Victory Parade through the streets of the town, marching behind the three Irish regiments. The Inniskillings, dressed in their saffron kilts and playing their bagpipes, led the parade.

The streets were dressed in bunting flags, and crowds of people were cheering and waving flags. In the high street, a kitten was running around, and it rushed straight under my feet and tripped me up. When we finally came to a halt in the park and were stood at ease, the junior Commander asked what caused the giggles. She was ahead and had no idea what happened, because she and the rest of the parade had to keep marching. I was the only one who was out of line and out of step for a few minutes, and quickly picked myself up and got into line and step. Anyway, everyone had a good laugh and so did I.

I remember August 15th 1945 very clearly, VJ Day (Victory in Japan). It was a beautiful sunny summer day and, in the lunch hour, I was lying on the grass bank in front of the mill. A Pioneer came running out from the mill calling to me "The war is over, the war is over. Here is your picture". He had just finished framing it for me. It was a little Irish picture I had painted and embroidered, and it hangs above my dressing table.

Keele

At the end of September 1945, we packed up to move to Keele when the Cypriot Unit moved out. There was a murder in the unit out there and so we unpacked again. We unpacked and packed up twice more, before finally moving there in November.

It was a large Stately Home, and our Irish Regiments were in huts around the park. The Officers' Mess was in the house, and our twenty four ATS girls were in the stable block, that was very nice once we got there. Every night and morning, we had to walk up and down a drive between very high rocks, and it was very creepy on dark winter nights.

While the Cypriots were here, there were two murders and a stabbing. They were a volatile lot, and so were the Irish, who drank too much and were always fighting each other. We girls stuck together and away from them as much as possible. We only went to the NAAFI on Friday lunchtime to buy things we needed - stamps, stationery, sweet ration, shoe polish, etc, and never socialised there.

The Vicar and his wife invited us for evenings with them by the fire with cups of tea and biscuits, that we enjoyed. It was nice to spend time with a family in their home. The long dark walk in winter through the park was not so good (it was like Knole Park in Sevenoaks). Saturday afternoons we went to Newcastle-under-Lyme to shop, or the cinema, and fish and chip tea. There was a lot of poverty, and we saw children without shoes in winter. It was awful.

We had a large fireplace in our room, where six of us slept and lived and spent most of our off duty time. We collected bits of wood for lighting the fire that we chopped with our dinner knives, and made a fire with any logs and coal that we could find. We also used to sneak from the cook house, tea, sugar and bread to toast, and anything we could to spread on it and any food we could lay our hands on, cake, etc. We used to buy Oxo, Bovril and Camp Coffee, and there was the occasional food parcel, so we did quite well.

We also collected fabrics, etc, and made toys that we sold to the soldiers for their children for Christmas, and the money we made went to charities, so we had cosy productive evenings round the fire. Peck, Marjorie and I were in the tailor's shop, and the other girls worked in various offices.

Our food was awful, but we were so hungry and often very cold, so we ate it. The potatoes were black and slimy, fried eggs were grey, and bacon was green, yellow and grey pink. It is a wonder it did not kill us all.

A Captain in the Orderly room organised trips to concerts at Hanley Town Hall, given by the Halle Orchestra and conducted by Sir John Barbirolli. We travelled standing in the back of a three-ton lorry, hanging onto a rope. The floor was metal. A cold uncomfortable journey, but the concerts were worth it. One evening, Isabel Bailey was singing, and several other soloists, players and singers, but their names escape me. One evening, we went to Manchester Opera House to see 'The Mikado'. It was a long ride but we enjoyed the light opera. There were usually about twelve of us on these jaunts.

Moving on

One winter evening, we returned to the billet from our tea in the cook house, and there, with standing orders on the notice board, were orders that we were moving. We had accumulated quite a lot of stuff for our handicrafts and toy making, and we had to pack everything that we had into our kit bag. No extra bags were allowed so we had to get rid of a lot of odds and ends.

Next morning, we received our posting orders and travel warrants, and we were dispersed around the country. Peck went to Guildford to be demobbed. Marjorie went to Wrexham, North Wales, and I went to Colchester, Essex. I lived in a flat in the married quarters with Jeanne who now lives in Cambridge, and we still write to each other. Peggy and Sybil we have lost touch with. There was another Victory Parade, and we marched all around the town with bands playing and crowds cheering and waving. There was also a similar parade when the Essex Regiment received the 'Freedom of the Town'. I have a newspaper cutting of this one.

There was also a huge Victory Parade in London, and everyone taking part was issued with a new uniform that often had to be altered, and new badges, stripes and medal ribbons stitched on. We were sewing these for weeks. Many of the badges were beautiful embroidery, some in gold and silver. There were four of us in the tailors shop, two were men, one from Yorkshire and the other a Jew called Samuel Fishbone, from the East End of London.

My next posting was to the tailor's shop in Maidstone Barracks, and I worked with an Irish girl called Mary who sang Irish songs all day. The main one being 'I'll take you home again Kathleen, across the Irish sea'.
    One afternoon, for P.E., we played hockey with mixed teams. My opponent was a mad Irish man, who rushed around swinging his hockey stick about like a shillelagh. I spent the whole of the game keeping out of his way to avoid being knocked round the head. We used to go to the ballroom at the Star Hotel to dances that we enjoyed very much, because they were never crowded or rowdy.

I then went to Canterbury for a very short while. On arrival, our workshop had not been set up and so we were allowed into town for a few hours. At the Cathedral, crowds had gathered to see the arrival of several Bishops with the Archbishop, and several Bishops from the Russian Orthodox Church.

Shorncliffe

From here, I went to Shorncliffe near Folkestone, my last posting. I was in the advance party, and it was winter. One afternoon, I was scrubbing a long corridor in the officer's mess with several others, when a cook came along with a pint mug full of hot thick and almost black tea for us. We stood in a circle, eight to ten of us, and passed it round, taking turns to drink. It tasted delicious.

The ATS were allotted the Cavalry Barracks for our quarters, and we were in some almost derelict huts in a muddy field. The floors were rotten, and sometimes our beds went through the floorboards. They really were appalling, and the weather was wet and cold. There were some new barracks up the road, and we sent a delegation to our Commander, and she eventually got us moved into the new barracks.

Late December 1946, it snowed and snowed, and froze until about March 1947. The miners went on strike, and we ended up with very little heating and hot food, and no water. Our barracks were situated on the cliffs above Sandgate and it was COLD.

We got boilers, those round stoves, and stoked them up. We had two of those in the barrack room, one at each end, to keep us warm. I'm not sure it was a good thing to have in a hut, keeping them stoked up, especially because of the coke fumes at night, surely it wasn't a good idea, but anyway we all survived.

Braving the cold at Shorncliffe during the winter of 1946-47.
I'm on the left in the front row

About 8pm, several of us would don our coats, scarves, boots and layers of clothes and run along the cliff road down into Sandgate, along the sea road and up Brewer's Hill back into barracks, and into bed while we were warm. It was the only way we could get to sleep. Our clothes were carefully folded under our mattress, to have some warmth in them to put on in the morning after washing in melted snow. Sometimes it was not melted properly.

There were hot drinks and cold food at the cookhouse (sandwiches, etc). Thank God, I had my little methylated spirit stove, with a little kettle and teapot. My friends and I blessed it. I used to fill a hot water bottle and walk around with it under my greatcoat. Restaurants in Folkestone used to give us hot meals for half price, and the Salvation Army canteen helped us.

Amazingly, we were all fit and we always found something to laugh about. Shorncliffe was alright, we were doing a lot of drill and tailoring, making sure the uniforms fitted properly.

Teaching

Shorncliffe was the headquarters of Army Education, and I applied to go on a teacher training course and got onto one quickly, put up one stripe and went to an army college at Chiseldon, in Wiltshire. It was a collection of huts set on treeless downs a few miles from Marlborough, and it rained for the month we were there in January, and it was bitterly cold. However, the college was well equipped with good teachers, and I enjoyed it. When I returned to Shorncliffe, I joined a Sergeant (Maria) in the school, and we taught girls returning from overseas.

In May 1947, I went on another course at Ledbury in Herefordshire, and we stayed at The Feathers Hotel in Ledbury. Each morning, we went to a large house round the corner for our lectures and lessons, that I thoroughly enjoyed. At the end of the course, I had to go before a Board in London for an interview. That went well, because I was promoted to Sergeant, so I had to look after about twenty girls or so, take them out on the square and drill them. I went back to the school in Shorncliffe to teach with Maria, who was de-mobbed in a few months, and then I was in charge.

At the beginning of June, I took the night train to Glasgow, where I was met the next morning and shown a few of the sights by a Transport Sergeant. In Sauchiehall Street, an old man was 'singing' mouth music. We met some more students and he drove us to the college. It was in Buchanan Castle near Loch Lomond, and it was lovely.

We had a wonderful library, lovely classrooms, excellent tutors and lecturers from Oxford and Cambridge, and a good social life. We all had to work incredibly hard, and we were all happy to get on with it.

Some weekends, we took our preparation and notes to Edinburgh, stayed in the Sergeants' Mess there and explored that lovely city. Sometimes, after Sunday lunch, we boarded the paddle steamer at Balmaha up at Loch Lomond while writing up notes, etc, had tea at the hotel and sailed back in the early evening. There were dances and Scottish balls in the ballroom, and on special occasions we could wear civvies. We also learned to take drill and parades.

At the end of September, we had our Passing Out Parade. Most of us had passed our teacher training course, and now we all went our different ways to teach.

Back in Shorncliffe, I moved out of the barrack room to a smaller one downstairs with three other Sergeants. Eileen was an Education Sergeant (like me) and I stayed with her in

Scarborough, her home. I was bridesmaid to Joan, and Mollie married Joan's brother, and we occasionally would meet up and always write at Christmas time. We lived in the Sergeant's Mess which was much nicer that the cookhouse and NAAFI.

Two evenings a week, I taught at Canterbury and did not get back to my quarters till midnight, and the third night was on duty until midnight and the next morning up at 4am calling the cooks and doing whatever was required until breakfast at 8am. I would teach until 5pm, so the days were long and busy, but I really enjoyed the life.

I met Ian Douglas here, he was our Pay Sergeant and now lives in New Zealand, and we still write. He visited us with Ngani, his wife.

Leaving the ATS

I served four and half years in the ATS, leaving in late 1949, and had bad times as well as good times. Lots of fun and experiences, and made lots of friends that I still have. I would not have missed those four and a half years for anything.

I had done my damnedest to get away from what I was already doing. I joined the services because I wanted to do something different, learn how to do that, but no, I could sew, so they kept me on doing that in the tailor's shop. If you go into something else you've got to be trained, and I'd already been trained in sewing. So I was sitting in the tailor's shop, doing that, altering uniforms with two other girls and doing that for my army life.

Army life was strict, but as long as you obeyed the rules, you were fine, and I enjoyed it, it was good. We got on all right, all the girls, we did our square bashing and all that sort of thing. You made good friends because you were living together and working together, and that was it. I became lifelong friends with Joan, Marjorie Rye, and Peck, her real name was Margaret, who married a Polish airman.

I hoped I would be travelling and see a bit of the country. Originally I was hoping I'd go abroad and see places abroad, but no, I kept trying to get places abroad, but I never made it. I did get based all over the country, and enjoyed seeing the country, because I was seeing parts of Britain that I wouldn't have seen, so I was enjoying that, and I got to Scotland, which I hadn't seen, and that was good.

In the end, I thought about it and realised that I'd got to come out sometime, and the longer I leave it the harder it would be, so I'd better get on with it and come out now. Coming out of the Army was quite difficult, trying to settle at home, because life was quite different and it was quite difficult.

More teaching

After the ATS, I ended up working at the Avalon Approved School in Chislehurst. In the ATS, in Scotland, I had joined the Army Education Corps and I did teaching there, needlework of course, and I enjoyed teaching and I wanted to teach, so I joined this approved school for teenage girls who were in trouble with the police, and I worked for the

Salvation Army, who ran the school. I was there for quite a long while.

I saw the Festival of Britain at Battersea Park, in 1951. I went with the Avalon girls and other staff to the South Bank to perform a dance.

In Battersea Park for the Festival of Britain in 1951

In 1953, Betty and I slept outside the Dorchester in Park Lane to see the Queen's Coronation. We were on the pavement under some trees, which was a blessing because it rained but they were in full leaf so they protected us from the rain, thank goodness. And we had a good view of the Queen!

Roy

My husband Roy was born in Hastings in 1927, and moved to Sidcup as a child, where he saw the fire at Alexandra Palace ('Ally Pally'), then he grew up in Ashford, where he could see the Battle of Britain taking place overhead.

As a child, he made a collection of hundreds of aeroplanes out of balsa wood, and had a whole collection of aeroplane spotter magazines. Roy loved cars, and built the family car, which was a 2 door sports car, which we called The Green Car.

The Green Car, built by Roy

He was in the Dental Corps of the RAF for his National Service until 1948, then he trained at London Polytechnic in photography and later joined the Ministry of Defence as a specialist high-speed photographer.

Roy went all over the place for the MoD, we never knew where he was or what he was doing. After working at

Pendine Sands in Wales, he was based at Fort Halstead (near Sevenoaks) from the mid 50's until the late 80's.

Courting and marriage

I first met Roy in Shorncliffe that awful hard long winter (1946-47). He was in the RAF Dental Corps at the time, and we met at a dance one night at the Leas Cliff Hall in Folkestone.

We continued to meet after that, we'd go to the 'flicks' as Roy would say, or run into each other at Leas Cliff Hall, or a dance hall behind Selfridges in London.

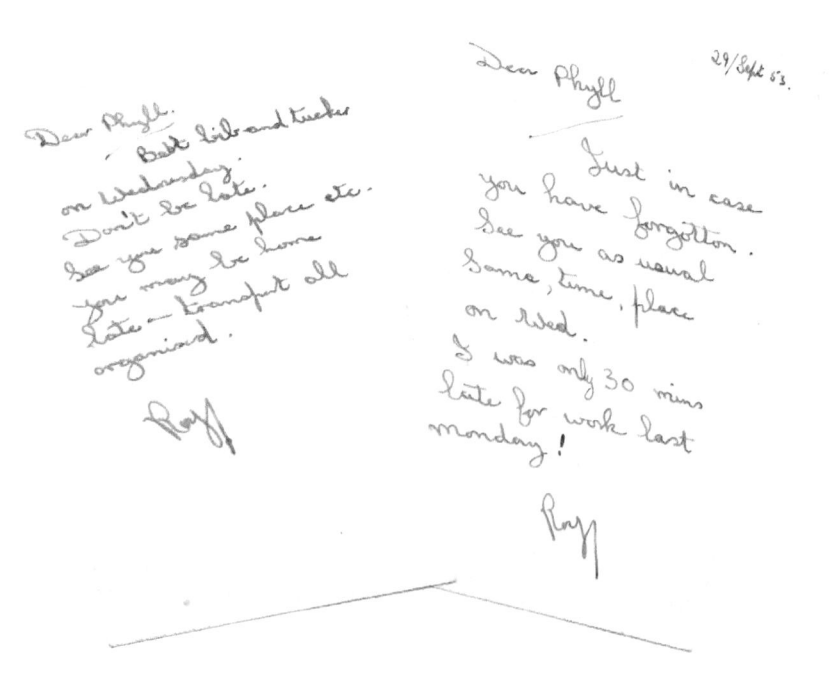

Letters from Roy arranging our Wednesday nights

Roy and I corresponded a lot, but it wasn't until 1950 that our regular 'Wednesday nights' began, meeting at 6.30 at Charing Cross. At the weekends, he used to drive down to see me or I would get the train from London to Wales, and that's how we had our time. Sometimes his car would break down and it would be difficult to meet, but we managed.

We took our time, and didn't get married until the mid 50's, when we'd saved up to buy a house. I did quite a bit of travelling in the meantime, all over the place, and I've always been independent, tried to earn my own money.

In the end, we decided to get married, on Wednesday of course, Wednesday 4th April 1956 in Keston Church.

We lived at Lennard Road in Dunton Green, and had Anne in 1961 and Sarah in 1967.

Our wedding day.
My Mother and Father are on the far right in the group photo

With Sarah (left) and Anne (right), as children, and at my 80th

Pictures from my later life

The Green Car - loaded up and ready for an adventure!

On a day out with Roy, visiting a local garden

I've always loved sewing and embroidery, even at 77!

I loved my garden, and enjoyed growing new plants from cuttings

Enjoying a trip to visit Sarah in Australia

Visiting the Biggin Hill Heritage Hangar in August 2014 with my daughter
Sarah and my grandson Charlie, still active and interested

With my grandson Charlie, swinging in 2017 and at Christmas 2021

Printed in Great Britain
by Amazon